TRUE DECEIT
FALSE LOVE

A Free-Verse Poetry Collection

Dr. Marni Hill Foderaro

Balboa Press books may be ordered through booksellers or by contacting:

Balboa Press
A Division of Hay House
1663 Liberty Drive
Bloomington, IN 47403
www.balboapress.com
844-682-1282

Because of the dynamic nature of the Internet, any web addresses or links contained in this book may have changed since publication and may no longer be valid. The views expressed in this work are solely those of the author and do not necessarily reflect the views of the publisher, and the publisher hereby disclaims any responsibility for them.

Any people depicted in stock imagery provided by Getty Images are models, and such images are being used for illustrative purposes only. Certain stock imagery © Getty Images.

ISBN: 979-8-7652-2603-2 (sc)
ISBN: 979-8-7652-2618-6 (hc)
ISBN: 979-8-7652-2617-9 (e)

Print information available on the last page.

Balboa Press rev. date: 03/19/2022

DISCLAIMER

The free-verse poems provided in this book and the writings in the TRUE DECEIT FALSE LOVE series of books are on an "as is" basis and intended for informational, educational and entertainment purposes only and should not be understood to constitute a medical, psychological or psychiatric diagnosis, healthcare recommendation or legal advice. The author's intent through these original poems is to build awareness and provide linguistic examples, definitions, descriptions and/or responses to understand and heal from the trauma of experiencing Domestic Violence, Narcissistic Abuse and/or Parental Alienation, as well as Intergenerational Family Trauma. The author and publisher make no representations or warranties of any kind with respect to the contents of this book and assume no responsibility for errors, inaccuracies, omissions or any other inconsistencies herein. Reading these terms, phrases, acrostic and free-verse poems are at your own risk and you agree to take full responsibility for any resulting consequences. The information in this book is not a substitution for direct expert assistance and may be triggering. Please seek legal advice or professional help from a medical, psychological, psychiatric or healthcare specialist if necessary. The author did not develop any of these terms and phrases, as they were coined by countless others, and is not an expert or licensed provider on Domestic Violence, Narcissistic Abuse, Parental Alienation and/or Intergenerational Family Trauma, is not responsible for any resulting consequences, and the use of this book implies your acceptance of this disclaimer. The opinions, roles and responses expressed in the poems are general and should not be confused with the opinions or experiences of the author. Certain agencies, businesses and professionals are mentioned for reference purposes only, however characters, roles, genders, locations, events and incidents are the products of the author's imagination. Any resemblance to actual persons, living or dead, male or female, young or old or actual events is purely coincidental.

When you eventually realize that you've experienced Domestic Violence, Narcissistic Abuse, Parental Alienation and/or Intergenerational Family Trauma, finding the language to understand what you've endured can be exceptionally challenging.

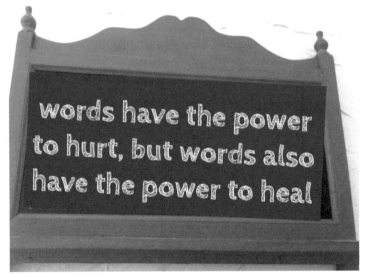

words have the power to hurt, but words also have the power to heal

Reading, writing and the process of creating poems can be extremely therapeutic on your healing journey as you make sense of trauma and connect the dots to your own experiences. Expressing yourself using the written word can aid in healing emotional wounds by externalizing your abuse and helping you understand your experiences, the malevolent perpetrator(s) and yourself better. Writing poetry provides much needed validation and allows you to release pain and process what you've been through, and sharing your ordeal through language can help provide inspiration to others in various stages of their own abuse recovery. In time, with inner reflection, you will come to understand the truth, find your survivor's voice, reclaim your authenticity and move towards living a blessed and happy life filled with abundance, gratitude and love.

AUTHOR BIOGRAPHY

Dr. Marni Hill Foderaro is an award-winning and celebrated author, speaker and educator. She earned her doctorate in education and completed postdoctoral studies at Harvard after a very successful and rewarding 35-year career as a high school Special Education Teacher, with 12 years as a university Adjunct Professor. Marni is the esteemed author of God Came to My Garage Sale, a 2020 Best Books award-winning Spiritual fiction and the 4-book series True Deceit False Love on Domestic Violence, Narcissistic Abuse, Parental Alienation & Intergenerational Family Trauma, all prominently endorsed. Marni is a lover of animals, nature, music and world travel and handles life's challenges with love and compassion. She values honesty, integrity, equality and goodness and prays for peace on earth. Marni was born in the South, raised her children in the Midwest and lives in the Caribbean. In addition to her speaking engagements and various writing endeavors on embracing Spirituality after surviving Family Violence, Marni is a contributing author to numerous anthology books, including: The Last Breath, The Evolution of Echo, We're All In This Together: Embrace One Another, Passing The Pearls, The Ulti-MUTT Book for Dog Lovers and volume 2 of bLU Talks Presents: business, Life and the Universe. In 2022, Marni was inducted into the Best Selling Authors International Organization. Dr. Marni Hill Foderaro's books, podcast and T.V. interviews, speaking engagements, book signings, guest articles and events can be found on her website.

www.GodCameToMyGarageSale.com

DEDICATION

To my wonderful, honest and loving life partner Rick

You know all the players and understand their games.

Thank you for your unconditional love and support as I navigate this often painful and heartbreaking earthly journey, and we both create a happy and beautiful life together in paradise.

I have been blessed beyond words to spend my days with you. The best is yet to come!

With so much love,

Marni

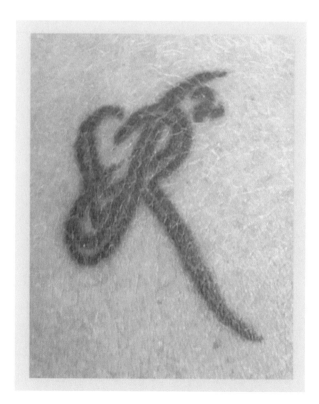

CONTENTS

Mama's Peas

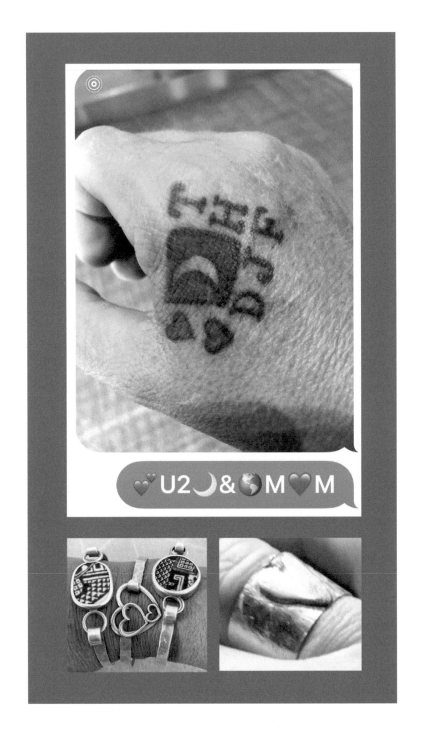

X

Cleveland Ohio Blues

Alex Bevan's Grand River Lullaby appears out of the blue, the Cleveland blue
Three C concert tour on an Ohio-bound college road trip, lined up for signed vinyls
Chubinupto my beautiful daughter? Too much lost time has passed since you put me up
I could buy you too with new, but choose to be HONEST, stay true and value a value or two

Remembering a cappella lullaby songs about wide waters, cherry stones and chicken bones,
Heartbroken because our story now has an end. Your Mama's left cryin' once again
They say love conquers all, unless the malevolent Alienator and Flyin' Monkey forces take hold
How can an innocent adult brain be washed, re-molded, taken hostage, split, bought and sold?

Our white porch swing sways, rocking my baby and her brother to sleep each night
Rhythm and rhyme, gentle tones and cool Midwestern breezes
Cuddled up in your Mickey blanket, holding your Cody bear tight, in a curled furl
so cozy, so cute, so secure, surrounded in love, my sweet little kiss girl

Never imagined back then you would stray, go away from your mother's loving arms
Signs abound and surround as I unwillingly surrender to reluctant acceptance, a sad life sentence
Ohio represents at the Livingston Taylor live online show, my Tuesday 11-time dueter of Loving Arms
and at Norma's STX Montpellier Domino Club with the drinking pigs, forced to correlate the two

The universe's signs and synchronicities continue to bite with Ohio's might
Shining the light, the white, the bright, the plight, now black as night
The baby pink, the light blue and now the very dark and gut wrenching blues
Les Cleveland blues, une Nor'easter moves

Left most of your childhood mementos with your alienating dad
Hoping that he'd save, not discard, your treasures so you'd know
And I flew personalized gifts and scrapbooks to you out East so you had
Your memories and some special treasures for friends you could show
I'm sure you're missing anything significant from me
Throwing out photos and gifts is a typical alienating strategy
Please know that your mom was the one who was always there for you
From the moment I learned I was pregnant with you, my love for you was true blue

The chime tunes, twelve NOONS on the clock's face, GRAFTIN' together time on the posts
Found your beautiful face illuminated by the backyard bonfire, circled with your new hosts
Scrolling, surfing, falling and landing. Going, going, gone my girl
I'll always remember you, the previous you, before reeling from your illegal dealing
Malevolent, evil Agent forces secretly moved you out of state, but first 'cross town
Stuck in the familiar hole, rabbiting down, tears flooding my gown, holiday frowns
Other players had a hand in the abuse, their "neutral" silence scream as alienation sounds

OPA! Kala Christougenna-Xronia Polla! The replacement family gathers at Annunciation
Ironic it's called The Great MOTHER Church; se AGAPO kori mou, my fili koritsi
Did you even remember your Targeted MOM lived in Greece? Nea Kiffisia, near Athens
Remember Baklava and Mom's Saganaki on fire? Memories rewritten to be falsely dire

Petitioned Blessed Archangel Gabriel, honored at the Synaxis, Hebrew salvation
Hope for communications, new beginnings and strength. Hope to again someday meet
No crown for Koumbara, a lifetime of Godmother's extreme deceit

A tabby's tail, a tall tale and twisted trail of calculated lies and betrayal
Can't sponsor my own blood, court-ordered silenced, resulting mute
Fear of reprisal, so can't send my love, holiday or birthday greetings or even a Hello
Sad truth is that we've all been Domestically Abused by your dad, my ex-mate
You've been brainwashed and taught to Hate, Decimate, that's your fate
Hoping you'll critically think. Why after so many years was your MOM at the brink?
Put two and two together. You can figure it out. You saw a lot with your own eyes.
Weiss in boots, puss in boots, shots in skis, art institute
Weiss, wise, whys...there there now, honor dishonorable lies

Stockholm Syndrome is real and a proven thing
Aligning with evil is part of the abusing alienator's operation sting
Independent Thinker Phenomenon makes you truly, but wrongly, believe
That you're the one deciding to estrange and to leave

Taking it to the level to cause my legal demise
The guilt you must feel when you finally realize
The damage you caused at court in the Pine Tree State
I pray for your soul to release you from your pain and hate
Forgive yourself because it's really not your fault
You've been used as a weaponized pawn to carry out this assault

CEO on his knee three times, no four, maybe more
Six children with number one, no number two, then return to number one
How publicly noble to prepare a bedroom for each. Typical playbook play
After bed, led and wed, left for dead, the doe show, his False Mask glows

Don't go OVER, stop and LOOK, or PARK, just DRIVE past the Guardians of Traffic
Drive past your maternal guardian who bore the door of two decades
More than a score, hearts forever bonded then tore, heads now sore to the core. No more
The shore, where the poor line the street. Preserving the integrity of the seawall
Videography of rushing wild water, following pa's patter, one of two aligned golden boys
Tears washed away like the big concrete slabs and stones on the movie reel, Lake Erie's deal

I pray to Saint Gerard, the Patron MOTHER of Saints.
They PREY to DAUGHTER Saint Gorgonia
Dimmon's not a Demon, and he surely wouldn't approve, veneration not vengeance for us
Seal the deal. Trying to heal. No betrothal, no service, no promise
Manageable Mirroring. An intergenerational curse. Stronghold mold I'm told.
Go from your narc dad one to his narc dad two. They both live untrue. Boo-hoo. I'm Blue

Life's like a play. Their facade and False Mask always slips. They can no longer hide
Break a leg, break your heart. Separate the boys from the girls. Stride. Take a side
Let go and let God. Forced to give up the fight. Goodbye. Good night. Take flight
Live with un-resolved LOVELESSNESS. At least try. Carry on. I accept my plight

I must rest and forge ahead. This is her journey now, not mine to don.
God's AGAPE Love will continue to see me through.
Negativity be gone. Sadly, but with a new purpose, I must sail on

This mother's love is eternally unconditional. Now I know why Granni was down
Even your beau's mum danced away. Fad—ING to BROWN
She was A-FORD—ed freedom, chose to BID-adieu, Tendu, flew and grew
I must fly too, far far away, but with tears in my eyes for the Cleveland Ohio Blues

ellie_the.tabby

Feline finally found. Adoption farce.
Tears ran dry, My oh my,
Confirmed her lie.
Her with Her-ley
Shame on she
Extorted, aborted
She's had a few
No value to life

We never really aligned
From the first of her many affairs
She lied, but I stayed by her side.
Trauma bonded since youth

She longed to be me.
I longed for stability.
Needs to be in control
Godmother's role
Knows better than all
Crossed boundaries.
Trail of betrayal.

Loyalty misguided
Condescending Projection
Intolerance if your opinions don't match hers
Stealing both of my girls

Did my fur-baby travel or stay? Keeping secrets at bay
Matching wool rugs took my breath away.
You aided alienation too. Shame on you.
Honesty is not a virtue you hold dear, dear.
Paws, Planned and a naughty pause. Using her claws.

The black panther hasn't a clue
A warrior she's called
Granni and her feline gone many moons
Boom Boom Sissy Boom Boom
The cat is out of the bag

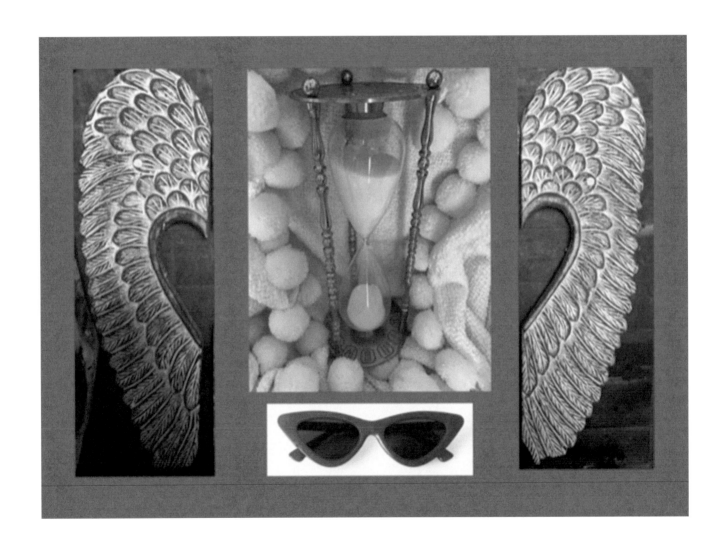

Vanished Voice

It happened so quickly and without warning. Unprepared.
No idea that would be the last time I heard her voice.
She coveted my perceived frolics and freedoms since youth
As she was stifled with fear, Pavlovian controlled
In the neighborhood her daily dinner bell rang and terror sang

Broken and coping, aborted babies, flirtatious indiscretions
Blame shifting projection, there there now she would say
Continued envy struck her superiority cord
She knew more than all, strength garnered in her stance
Behind the curtain, the deceitful and all-knowing Oz evolved

Trauma bonds formed unawares, mistaken for sisterhood
Intolerance, Belittling and calls for Branding. The control and cover up.
Closure not needed or yearned. The painful life lessons learned
My voice ceased following her lead, no need, no plead, her deceitful greed
No hard choice when up high on the watershed, staring at the fork in the road
My lightbulb was clearly illuminated. Dark-hand's shifty disquiets
Calm denial during her Rockstar riots

One word was a game changer and jolted my reality: "Condescending"
The projection was crystal clear Missy. Your supply ran dry. Goodbye
Waterfalls and floods ensued, but a strong resolve unfolded
So done with your deceitful betrayal, so done with being scolded

The abrupt ending of a lifelong friendship with your "best friend."

Secret Agent Man code

6BDHF1 don't tell 5BDNJJ7 or 6BDTAR0

Juggling Supply while married

The Half-Brother

De-Paul Mench mentor, Chi-town boy
Son of God, son of who? Don't be coy

Paternity test confirmed, who knew?
Hide the truth, so many cheaters do

Secrets kept, with my husband she slept,
Talmud, Torah, the kids and I wept

Familiar and familial facial features
We are all, even sinners, God's creatures

It's surely a brotherly match
Tough truth to swallow down the hatch

Followed the hunch
Confirmed the punch

Took the Georgia midnight train
Embraced Power, not deceitful pain

ROLSIES

April Showers; Mother May I Flowers?

She spews in pews
The facade front fans
Flying Monkeys, songs and musical bands

Delicious deceit, deliberate, delusional, demented
Basement finger frolics with the other D-girl, another Miss Bi
I kept your secret while you were paid to play ma, or tried

Align with evil as you stir your oatmeal 'round
Caught you at a cornerstone, that's where you were found

Had Faith in your friendship, as many people do
I was fooled, future-faked, bought out; you were not true

My tears were streaming as the graduates turned the page
inside screaming while online streaming as MY child crossed the stage
You took my place as the Hawks' tassels turned
Shame on you nanny, her real Mom was burned

You hide behind religion but there's no doubt
That God knows who the sinners are and what you're all about

They'll be no knight in shining armor
Just a very dishonest little prince
It's a dog-eat-dog world, never heard from you since

Waking From The American Dream

My dream came true, 2.5 children and a garden with a gazebo
Our white picket-fenced home was completed
All my hopes were realized and for years life was carefree, yet faux
I had no idea that my false fairytale would all be deleted

Over pizza one night at the local pub I froze
My world came to a crashing end
Confessions were made and wrongdoings exposed
So severe that there was no way to mend
Stunned into silence trying to comprehend the betrayal
Connecting the dots of deceit
Then shoved against a wall, followed by angry threats
I knew I had to escape, leaving my tree-lined street
Predators usually don't let their prey go easily
I wrongly thought he would do what's right
No, he needed to destroy me and take everything away
That's when he ramped up his sadistic fight

However, abusers misjudge the strength and resolve
Found deep in the soul of their victim spouse
In time my life improved significantly
Even though he stole the kids, money and house
Abusers can take it all, just like the Grinch
But we know what really matters is Love
Love can't be destroyed by evil forces that flinch
Because survivors can and do rise above

Marvelous Maine made by M♥M

Euphoria's Escape

Ephemeral Euphoria, like Saint Euphemia
Love bombed and twirling, Effortless
Setting the table, sending out holiday cards, trimming the tree
The stockings are hung by the chimney with glee
Happy, content, complete, let's toast...cheers
well-spoken, cool and confident, no tears and no fears

Go through the motions
Living the dream
Keeping it all together
While the evil one schemes

Narcissistic Abuse creeps
The hostess retreats
Not good enough anymore
Gaslit and questioning
Ignore the confusion and each Red Flag
No longer capable or worthy, just a discarded hag

Martyrdom looms
Careful what you say
Fear, gloom and doom
Vigilant observances
Legal threats are all they have.
When they can't control you
They control how others see you

Lost all support
Nowhere left to turn
Run for your life
Heal from the burn

Scarred, marred but free
The cost is too high for me

Lucky to escape
But it came with significant loss
The abuser's warnings fulfilled
Those threatening promises kept
Time to move away and move on
Too many fears and tears wept

ERASED MOM

Perverted Purpose

Severing mom's loving parent-child bond is dad's number one goal
His life's purpose now is to track and to troll

While he hides behind a mask playing victim, playing dumb
Making our kids dependent, trauma-bonded and numb

Trying to breathe, collect myself and find my voice
Avoiding triggers if and when there's a choice

Posted photos online of storybook smiles
Intact families gathered 'cross the many miles

Generations should be true and celebrate
Show love and forgiveness, not abuse or hate

My holidays are now spent quietly alone
No cards, visits, calls or texts on the phone

Lost hopes, expectations and fairytale dreams
All because one sick child-abusing alienator schemes

Hiding behind a false persona and mask
It's his mission now, his full-time task

Filing bad faith court petitions is all he has left
To keep me connected after all of his theft

Secret Agent addictions will keep him in debt
Pornography and Gambling, didn't know when we met

Turning a corner and coming to terms
I'm a survivor, oh yes, I'd like to confirm

We all have a journey on this earthly plane
I live with compassion and not with disdain

God knows the truth and has filled me with love
I continue to pray for peace and follow the dove

Injustice Revealed

Now the entire world can understand the Targeted Parents' plight
We've seen so much Corruption and Fraud on a global scale
Shocked by deceit as they don't do what's right
So how can legal justice ever prevail?

Family Court can be a profitable enterprise
Children are often used as pawns for continued abuse
Some lawyers lie as Judges rule in favor of the one in disguise
The alienators' big bucks and connections tighten the noose

Targeted Victims are often re-abused in court
Told "truth will prevail" and "You can trust us"
Unethical and Ineffective lawyers can and do extort
Even if they write a book about equal justice

So many families suffer and are torn apart
It doesn't have to be this way
If you realized the evil right from the start
Then you could have been free today

Now our children have lost me because of you
They have both been taught to hate
And they've lost half of themselves and are living untrue
Because of one malevolent ex-mate

It is all about you; don't you see what you've done?
What has happened to you and our two?
Narcissists breed narcissists, and narcissists shun.
I pray for you all, but must bid adieu.

Unleash Your Burdens

Three decades young and struggling
When life should be carefree
You've been isolated and controlled
Wishing you could feel worthy

You're handsome, kind and funny
And very, very smart
Please don't align with evil
Which alters your loving heart

Wish your beautiful eyes would open
Understand and have a clue
And gain self-sufficient independence
So you can live a life that's true

The power is in your hands
To unleash your burdens and be free
There's so much beauty in the world
Yet you choose virtual reality

Explore your new Frontier
You have everything you need
Hope you hold your loved ones dear
With gratitude you'll succeed

You moved to the sea and sun
To start fresh and to start anew
But you're missing out on tons of fun
SoFlo has many great things to do

You have the power to change
Yet keep both parents in your life
My heart broke when you estranged
As it cut me like a knife

Guiding you on your path too many times
God knows this mom has tried
Just to see you self-sabotage
Too many tears I've cried

Wounded souls can heal
But it takes a strong resolve
To get off the spinning wheel
And work hard to evolve

You can take the needed steps, don't fall
It's like climbing a tall tree
To realize your potential
And be the best that you can be

In my heart I know you can
Save your soul and release the strife
Now that you're a grown man
Only you can save your life

A mother's love is true
And is to the moon and back
Reminded by our tattoo
Hope you get yourself back on track

Please take care of yourself and know
You are worthy just as you are
We're all on this journey to grow
Happiness can be near not far

You have the power to survive
If that is what you want to do
You can enjoy life and thrive
But now it's totally up to you

Seeing The Forest For The Trees

"Oh c'mon; you're overreacting."
"Don't be so sensitive."
"I have IN EFFECT told you that I was mistaken."
"Put it behind you."
"You heard me wrong."
"You SURELY can't blame me for having affairs; your mother was so very ill."

Exact words that were spoken
Prefaced by a token of
Love Bomb words of praise
To create the planned haze
After yet another discounting
Of your daughter who has only wanted your love

At first I bit my tongue
When the liar called ME dishonest
Projection at its finest, now I finally see
As the inevitable unfolded
Still hurt to hear
From the parent who molded
My thoughts and actions
Which led to the patterns
Generational grooves
Taking eons to prove

Hard knocks from this plane
Disdain, vain supply gained
Gaslighting technique to question if sane

You pushed mom off the bridge as she attempted suicide many times
And had her involuntarily committed in locked psych wards
Shock Treatment, Affairs, Parental Alienation and courthouse crimes
Putting us kids on the stand, re-abusing her with your malevolent swords

The lonely confusion and continued efforts failed
Not this time, too much and too late, the truth was unveiled
Envy's ugliness entailed, but still caught me by surprise
But now honesty and goodness must prevail
You'll always justify your abuse and your lies

We all make time for what's important to us
Your actions speak louder than words
Gang up on the broken, the truth has been "spoken"
Much too late for our troubled Jaybird

I understand now Mama
60 years way too late, since
You've crossed the bridge
And went through Heaven's Gate

I will stop this Intergenerational Trauma Cycle
Even though it hurts my heart to estrange
But done for the right reasons of honesty and goodness
I'm compelled to make this hard change

I've tried for years to be extremely generous
Reaching out with a trip and gifts from the heart
Narcissists are innately venomous
So our unaligned values will keep us apart

You'll brush this off and have another drink
Your victim narrative will likely not alter
Almost a century of blame shifting and projection
It's on me because, of course, you would never FAULT-er

I never seem to be or do enough
I have loved you all these years
Your dismissive responses hurt so much
As I'm always left in tears.

I could go along status quo or try to confront
But I'd be met with denial, your "SNIDE" response would be blunt
Don't need more years of triggers and abusive remarks
I don't deserve that treatment from you or any narcs

I now see the Forest for the trees
Safe on my island with the Caribbean breeze
Taking a stand and doing what's right
After so many years, giving up the painful fight.

BOB

Caribbean Calls

Move on, move out, move away
Far away to an island getaway
Out in the open, but protected
Secluded, safe, surrounded by the beautiful sea
Winds of change, blowing steady for me

Finding my voice through my yen and my pen
Halted life stopped in a day, in a daze
Where days turn to months and months turned to years
Mustn't fear, God's love is dear and near

Salt, sun and sea, I'm on a great track
Securely sheltering in place, time to release
New love found and adventures distract
Helping me move towards calm and inner peace

Manifested support came to me
At Sandy Point floating, Oh Glory be
Maybe this time justice will prevail
And the sociopath will finally lose the wind in his sail

Stalking and talking
As he continues his quest
I choose to live life best
Away from the rest

It's time now to let me go.
Focus on your new home, new job and new doe
Who knew? Our next door neighbor for years
Done with you and the fears, dried up are the tears

Been given a second chance
To experience the dance
I've created a beautiful life
Away from the pain and strife

I Am

Untethered and free
Took many years and many tears
Honoring I, myself and me
Finally learned to face my fears

I can't control others
Nor do I want to, let them be
I did my best as a loving mother
At fault that I didn't foresee

The sociopathic narcissist, to save his face
Ramped up his abusive game
He stole money, assets and our foreclosed place
But that wasn't his biggest aim

Abusers conquer, destroy and are cunning cons
So they steal what means the most
Your children are used as weaponized pawns
Abusers' lies win in court so they can boast

Our brainwashed kids aligned with their dad
Because they're bought off and live in fear
Inside their hearts they're broken and sad
Deep down they want their loving mom near

Stockholm Syndrome deeply sinks
So kids don't Independently Think
A researched phenomenon
Losing your children in a blink

Big differences in both parents
Shown by actions, not by words
The contrast is apparent
you've been abused and you've been lured

Narcs lie, cheat and steal
That's part of who they are
Projection so they feel
Like they're the shining star

I've tried hard to reach out
The best that I can
Our lives have been altered
From the original family plan

Immersed in the absolute beauty
A tropical island can provide
Blessed to have found love and light
I now take my life in stride

Writing heals and tears have dried
I speak the truth and found rebirth
Hoping your all-black-and-white Splitting will subside
And you realize the truth, your value and worth

I know that I'm not perfect
I don't profess to know it all
Just following my gut and heart
And tearing down the wall

Expectations have been lowered
So I can survive day to day
No more unfulfilled resentments
Best to let go, let God and pray

Truth and goodness must prevail, it's true
The lion is not a lamb
Mom's honesty has always been woven into
The fabric of who I am.

Just as the Caribbean-African stilt-dancing Moko Jumbies found healing with awareness, perseverance and freedom, so have I. "Moko" means HEALER and "Jumbi" means SPIRIT. And just like the Mokos, I have always been drawn to bright, ethnic, colorful clothes. The Mokos traditionally were like Gods who watched over villages, with the ability to foresee danger and evil. As a survivor, I too am now more discerning about who I let into my life. In current times, Moko Jumbies have evolved and are on hand for Carnival and other celebrations. I have been given the opportunity to start anew and celebrate blessings on my earthly journey. Through the pain and significant losses I have endured as a result of being targeted, I see hope and possibilities, and I will follow my earthly path with LOVE, honesty, compassion and goodness in my heart. I will fill the rest of my days living with GRATITUDE.

Call
your mother.
Tell her you
love her.
Remember,
you're the only
person who
knows what
her heart
sounds like
from the
inside.

KEEP
CALM
AND
CALL
MOM

M♥M LOVES YOU!

Check out the other books in the series

TRUE DECEIT
FALSE LOVE

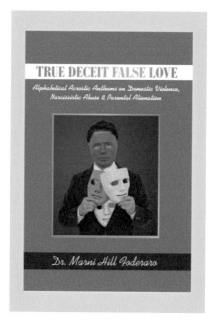

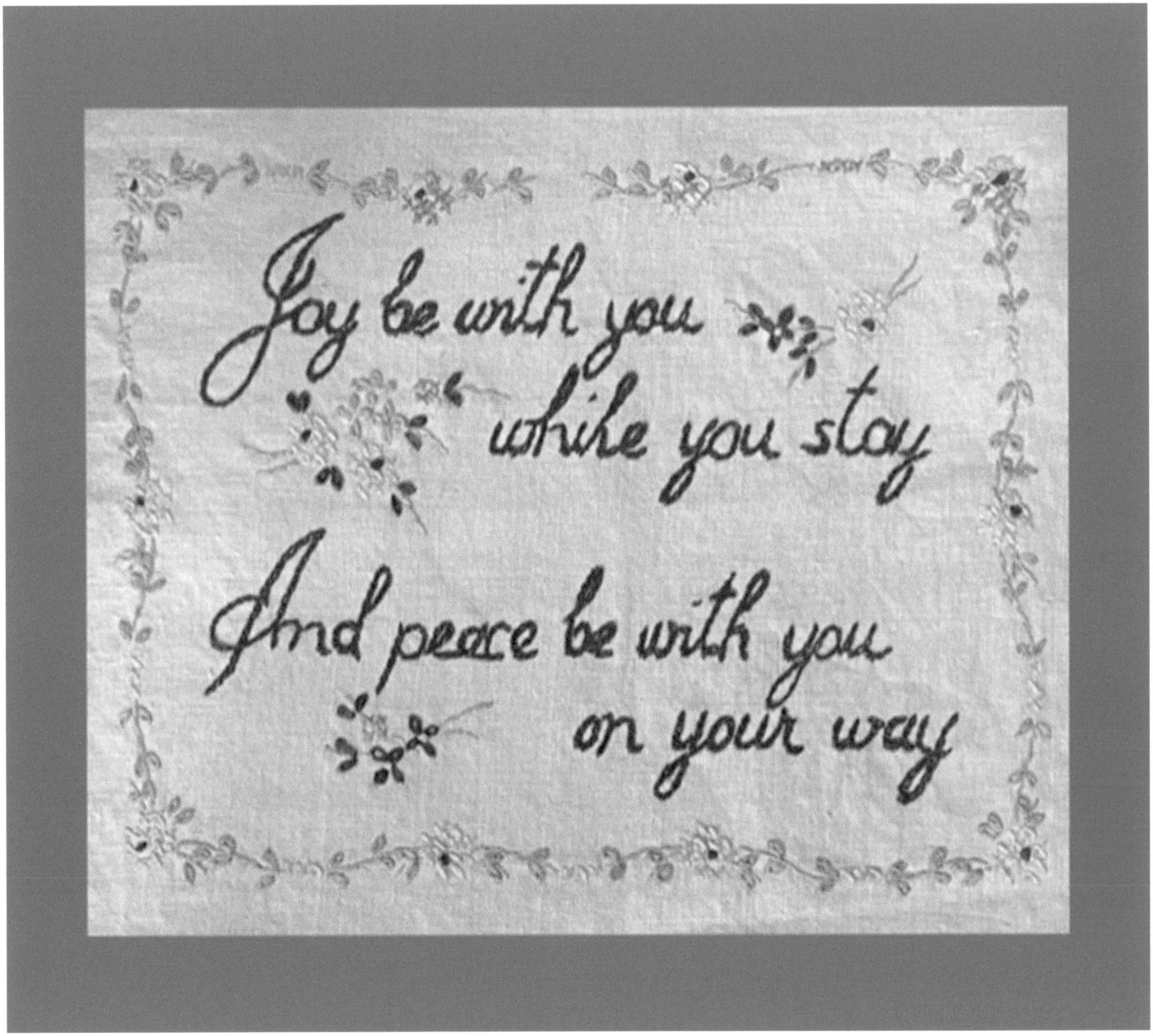
Joy be with you
while you stay
And peace be with you
on your way

Printed in the United States
by Baker & Taylor Publisher Services